# My
# Colorful
# World Travels

My

# Colorful

# World Travels

Written by Aarush Nishant Tilak
Illustrated by Parisa Cheraghi

ZOUEV PUBLISHING

This book is printed on acid-free paper.

Illustrations by Parisa Cheraghi

Published 2017
ZOUEV PUBLISHING
Printed by Lightning Source
ISBN 978-0-9934187-2-3, hardcover

"During our frequent countryside walks, my parents and I would enjoy watching large flocks of birds migrate to destinations all over the world to ensure their survival, without any restriction of borders. Every time I witness this natural phenomenon, I believe these birds remind us that the world is one land that God meant to be home to us All."

I dedicate this book to my dearest Mom and Dad who, since I can remember refer to me as their "treasure."

And to all children in our beautiful and colorful world!

# Introduction

My name is Aarush and I am from the Netherlands. I am ten years old and I have lived in many countries all over the world as my parents work for the United Nations. These countries include Iran, Syria, France, Switzerland, Niger, Djibouti, Rwanda and Bangladesh. I have, therefore, been to many schools and made friends of diverse cultures.

One of the important facts of life I have come to realize over the years is that to receive love, parental attention, care, and education often is a matter of sheer luck for many children all over the world. I have learned that to be rich or poor, or to be safe and in good health, to be confined to a wheelchair (if at all your family can afford one), or to be well-cared for or either having to beg in the streets; this all depends on the cradle you happen to be born in - a matter over which no child has any control.

During my travels, I have met children who had very loving parents but who simply were so poor that they slept in the streets in a make-shift home and had to go out begging in the streets to survive. For such children playing or going to school remains a remote dream. On the other hand, I have also met some kids with well-off parents who were craving for their busy parents' attention. I therefore think that the key ingredient for a truly happy child is to be able to go to school and to be cared for by loving, attentive parents.

I had been thinking about how I could express my gratitude for my happiness and privileged experiences. So I thought of writing some of my experiences in this small booklet which I wish to dedicate to all the children in our colorful world.

I want to tell them through this contribution that we should care about each other and that I have come to realize after having lived in so many different countries and cultures, that we are all so much alike, I believe that what in fact makes us so special to one another, is our distinct rich cultures and traditions. We should, therefore share our ways of life more with one another to further deepen our friendship. This book is part of that attempt to deepen our common friendship.

This is a booklet about experiences, traditional festivals, ceremonies and practices I learned about and found to be educational, funny, interesting, and sometimes even mysterious. I am aware that this booklet is a very small contribution, but I hope deeply that it shall symbolize a seed that will serve as an inspiration to many other people and underline the message that we are all ONE family that can learn so much from one another. The proceeds of this booklet will serve to support charity projects promoting children's awareness, the preservation of their environment, and the needs of mentally challenged children. For more information please visit: www.AarushGreenFarm.org

# Chapter One - Iran

## The Fire Festival

I was very young when we lived in Iran. My mom told me that as my nanny was Persian, I picked up the Farsi language in no time which I have sadly lost throughout the years except for a few words. Iranian people are very kind, generous and lively and this is reflected in their many joyous festivals.

A festival which we celebrated each year was the 'fire festival' called *CHARSHANBE SURI* on the last Tuesday of December. This is a very cool tradition where people set up bonfires in the streets and jump over them as a symbolic gesture to cleanse themselves of all the misfortunes and impurities of the past year, and to prepare themselves to welcome the coming new year which is called Nowruz. Seeing adults and even kids jumping over bonfires is great fun, while this is always done under the watchful eye of an adult.

# End of New Year

Another fun event which my family and I very much enjoyed was joining in the SIZDAH BEDAR festival which takes place on the 13<sup>th</sup> day of the Persian New Year, marking the closure of the New Year. This festival is all about spending a fun and happy time outdoors with family and friends, enjoying picnics and playing games in which even the adults take part. Indeed, big folks! No laptops and mobile phones allowed on this day!

This fun time goes on all day while people play music and dance, enjoying the warmer temperatures of a new spring! The picnic items set out traditionally include yummy foods like grilled kabobs, chicken with rice and beans, and *Ash-e Reshteh*, which is a noodle soup made with chopped spinach, parsley, and kidney beans, while various Iranian snacks, colorful sweets and fruits are part of the delicious menu!

People of Iran give great importance to these festivals because they keep ties with family and friends very strong.

I may have been very young, but I surely do miss those times with our Iranian friends!

# Chapter 2 - Switzerland

## The Escalade

Switzerland is not only a country of extraordinary scenery, hills and mountains. The Swiss also enjoy very rich and diverse traditions as they originate from several different cultures. The country therefore has no less than three official languages namely French, German, and Italian.

While we lived in Geneva, every year we enjoyed the great historical festival of the Escalade in the hilly old town center of Geneva. The Escalade commemorates the victory over invading troops in 1602 as the city came under a surprise attack at night by a large army of mercenaries sent by the Duke of Savoy who wanted to re-conquer the city.

When the attack was discovered by a young woman, she poured boiling vegetable soup over the soldiers from her window which awoke other residents. As the battle erupted, the Genevans courageously took up the fight with everything they could find at hand to defend the city including chairs, tables and rifles. Eventually, they managed to defeat the Savoyard invaders.

It is thus the courage of the Genevans for having themselves defended the city which is abundantly being celebrated each year. This traditionally goes with lots of stands where hot vegetable soup is served in the old town, together with many other goodies such as handmade small chocolate pots decorated with the red and yellow Geneva colors, and topped with colorful marzipan vegetables.

During this festival, children dressed in 17th century outfits collect coins after singing Escalade songs in the squares, restaurants or at your door, for a variety of charities.

At the end of the festivities, the tradition is that a large chocolate marmite gets smashed by the youngest and oldest participants, while reciting words of victory.

# Chapter 3 - France

## Buche de Noel

We all know that French cuisine is appreciated all over the world, but I wonder how many people know about the Yule log which is a deeply cherished French tradition going back centuries and commonly celebrated during Christmas. It was about families decorating a strong tree trunk with ribbons which would burn up gradually, keeping them warm during the extreme cold days, almost similar to how people today would decorate a Christmas tree.

As modernization set in over the following centuries and the tradition of the Yule log became outdated, the French came up with a recipe to replace this old tradition with a modern dessert recipe today called 'Buche de Noel,' which truly resembles an edible log decorated nicely with confectionary sugar to resemble snow.

The Buche de Noel is often prepared by children during Christmas. As I started my schooling in France, we prepared this very tasty cake during Christmas with our teacher and succeeded quite well! I can recommend to all the boys and girls to try this out under the guidance of an adult.

# Chapter 4 - Rwanda

## UMUGANDA

Rwanda is a landlocked East African country where Umuganda is a popular community-based activity which takes place on the last Saturday of every month. In this event, adult residents of the neighborhood join in to clean and tidy the neighborhood. Umuganda literally means: 'together to achieve an outcome'.

I remember well how Fred, our domestic helper, together with dad and mom would take part while always carrying some gardening utensils with them. As I was too small to help, I would then watch them from my little garden treehouse together with my pet rabbit Snug and our dogs Clifford and Whistle.

Umuganda is a practice in which expats could optionally participate alongside government officials and local population to serve this important community activity which was at times encouraged by the president himself! It was nice to see people connecting and working together for their neighborhood while having lots of good laughs.

Rwandans actually try in many ways to keep the environment clean. Bringing plastic into the country is, for example, strictly prohibited and everything is therefore placed in paper bags. Thumbs up for Rwanda in setting a great example in keeping our beautiful world healthy for all life!

# Beauty and Respect for Balance of Nature

While living in Rwanda, we visited many beautiful places, but my favorite weekend destination by far was Gisenyi, a little paradise located in the western province of this awesome country and very close to the Congolese border.

It was incredibly exciting to wake up at dawn with my dad to watch the sunrise from the shores of Lake Kivu, while we could see in the far distance local fishermen returning with their overnight catch as they chanted truly captivating tunes in perfect harmony. In these early hours we could also see the local women tidying the premises of their humble homes while children were enjoying their baths near the lake's shore.

I remember so well how the refreshing early morning breeze and the smell of the air, together with the lively sounds of nature awakening, blended so perfectly with the tunes chanted over and over again by the fishermen. These amazing experiences made me realize how connected we all are to nature and that probably nothing in this world could overtake the happiness lived by these hard-working and peaceful fishermen of Gisenyi.

# Chapter 5 - Djibouti

## Refugee Children

While in Djibouti, a little country in East Africa, I much enjoyed travelling with my parents to discover desert life. If we would travel early enough, we would be lucky to see large monkey families sitting alongside the roads well before sunrise. The tiny fluffy babies' clinging to their mothers bodies was the cutest sight!

At times my mom took me along to visit the crowded camps where families fleeing war lived in tent-like shelters and where I saw many children like myself who enjoyed playing and doing all the fun things a kid likes to do. I did not speak their language, yet we understood our gestures as they proudly showed me their self-made toys which they generously offered me to play with.   I thought they were probably much more attached to these toys than the ones I simply bought in the toy shop.   I hardly understood why these kids with so much creativity can just be called 'refugees'.

Back on the road, camels were a normal everyday sight which I found exciting every time I saw them! Their height was breathtaking, and it was funny how they always seemed to be chewing on something tasty with their poorly brushed teeth as they make their way. Another thing I found truly amazing was to see little goats climbing and spending a good share of their day in trees!

It appears they can do this thanks to their cloven hooves that help them to balance on centimeters-wide ledges and their powerful legs can propel jumps of nearly as high as twelve feet! It is said that they climb the trees to find fruits but also to find shade in Djibouti's hot and desert climate. I could go on writing about Djibouti as it is in one of the poorest yet one of my most favorite countries we lived.

## Popular Passing of Time

Djibouti is a small very hot country where we lived for one year. I was surprised to see the poverty in this country and how difficult life was for the average Djiboutian. I remember well that traffic lights were being introduced for the first time in the capital just as we arrived in 2013.

Soon we also came to find that due to the hot desert climate, a green medicinal plant with mild intoxicating properties called KHAT proved a very popular activity for both Djiboutian men and women. Khat chewing was often taken with some soft drinks to further reinforce its effects. It has a history as a social custom dating back thousands of years!

# CHAPTER 6 - Bangladesh

## The Kite Festival

Cox's Bazar is a town in southeastern Bangladesh where I lived for two years. I was lucky to enjoy many cultural festivals in which children take an important place, like the annual kite festival. In Bengali it is called the 'Shakrain' festival, dating from the Moghul period while it is one of the oldest festivals symbolizing unity and friendship in some South East Asian countries including Nepal and India. The kite festival takes place at the end of the cold season (cold enough to wear winter jackets and thick woolen vests!), along Cox's Bazar's beautiful natural beaches stretching over some 120 kilometers and known to be one of the largest beaches in the world!

This festival involves the whole family and is a very colorful and joyous event where young and old display and compete in exciting kite "fighting", with kites of all names, shapes and designs either on the beach or from people's rooftops, while children firmly believe that their wish expressed while launching their kite will undoubtedly come true.

The celebrations go on until late night with fireworks and countless colorful paper balloons lighting up and decorating the sky, while artists perform their flame-blowers acts and families enjoy music, popular dances and the different kinds of rice cake, dishes and pastries prepared for this joyous event.

# The struggle to preserve the Mother Tongue

I also learned about the International Mother Tongue Day while in Bangladesh, as this country played an essential role in its international recognition. Many people do not know that 21st February was declared International Mother Tongue Day in honor of Bangladeshi University students who had created a Language Movement but were killed in efforts to maintain their mother tongue, Bengali, as one of the country's official national languages.

The Language Movement built on the spirit to defend the rights to write in one's mother language. On this day therefore, Bangladesh and all other countries worldwide extensively celebrate their culture and ancestral language.

I believe that struggling to preserve your mother tongue makes complete sense, as I do not believe that anyone can express themselves better than in their mother tongue. I therefore believe it is beautiful that this day is celebrated by people throughout the world. After all, every mother tongue is invaluable as it carries an important cultural heritage that is passed on from generation to generation.

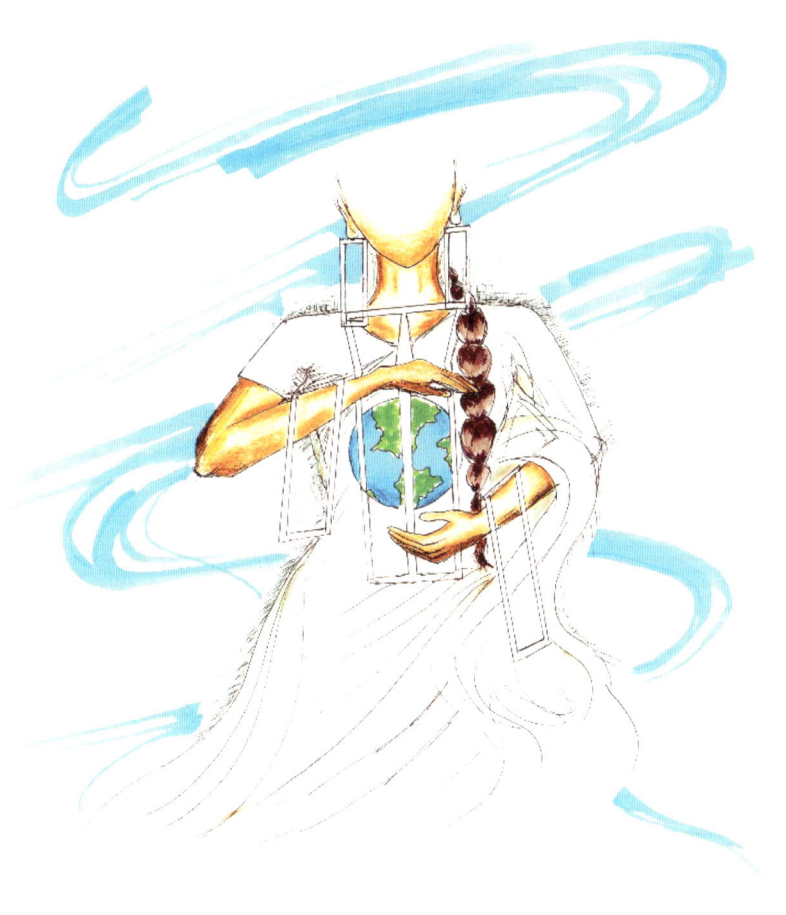

# Chapter 7 - India

## Life-lasting Bond Between Brother and Sister

In the Hindu tradition worldwide, family relations and unity between siblings are carefully fostered through the annual festival of *Raksha Bandhan* which in Sanskrit literally means "the tie or knot of protection". It is an ancient Hindu festival still very much intact today that ritually celebrates the love and duty between brothers and sisters.

In Hindu families, this deep affection between brothers and sisters is celebrated where brothers offer their blessings to their sisters, while sisters tie a colorful bracelet (called a RAKHI) around the brother's wrist and symbolically feed him delicious dairy based Indian sweets to mark this ceremony of bonding and life-lasting affection between the siblings.

However, the brother is not off the hook unless he offers some nice gifts to his loving and (as some of my friends told me), at times demanding sisters! I don't know who invented this festival but feel that although I don't have a sister, no matter how much a sister may be a pain at times, deep down, it certainly must feel very good to have them around.

# The Colorful Spring Festival

One of the most amazing colorful festivals celebrated by Hindus all over the world is the Holi festival (also called Holika or Phagwa). It is an annual festival celebrated on the day after the full moon in the Hindu month of Phalguna (early March) in which everyone, no matter what caste, status, religion, age or gender, abundantly joins in.

Holi welcomes the coming of a new spring, throwing off the gloom of winter time. Every time I witness this festival, it feels as if the most colorful rainbow descends on Earth and makes people miraculously forget about all their worries.

The rejoicing and merrymaking of people during the Holi festival can also be explained by its spiritual significance of the victory of good over evil. This is why, at the end of the first day of the festival a bonfire, at the rising of the moon, is made in which the evil demon is symbolically set on fire.

As the Holi festival of colors and joy aims to bridge social gaps and bring people together, I wished it would be celebrated by all people worldwide to bring nations closer together as a colorful symbol of universal friendship and peace.

## The Ritual of the Wanzam

While living in Niger, a landlocked country located in West Africa, I enjoyed playing with local kids when I got back from school. One day, a 15 year old boy told me of a tradition he went through as a kid, when he was 9 years old, just a bit younger than me today. He told me of a special ceremony which took place in his ancestral village for a dozen boys including himself.

He described that the boys were all dressed clean in white Boubou (traditional clothing) as if they were going for the Friday prayers. Only on this day they were dressed for a very important traditional ceremony that was to take place for each and every one of them. Some of the boys, he remembered, had joy and pride in their eyes, but in others he could also read intense fear for what was about to happen.

It was a big happening that was essential to be celebrated by all relatives and other villagers, including parents, adolescents, and adults. My friend told me that in African tradition, all elders are very happy on this day, and that in the eve, families had already purchased chickens, guinea fowl, and meat to abundantly celebrate the occasion and offer gifts for the ceremony. The boys were brought to a man called the "Wanzam" which means "traditional circumciser". The rituals conducted by the Wanzam embodied the passage to adulthood.

The boys sat with pride before the Wanzam, who started conducting some rituals, before he, with his sharp blades, excised them one by one. Some would cry out of pain, but my friend said that the more courageous remained calm which was seen as a sign of pride by the whole village and whose bravery is recounted throughout the year under the Palaver trees, recalling that "he is a true man, he did not cry". These boys, who were considered children moments back, were now seen with pride as young men in their village.

The face of the boy sharing the story held a constant expression of satisfaction while sharing his experience with me. I also believed that he may well have been among those who did not cry.

However, my friend's face looked more serious as he concluded that these rituals gradually are disappearing in today's Niger as the Wanzams start to work more with the medical clinics, so that infections and other unwanted problems for the kids can be prevented. As for the elders, they continue to speak of these ancestral traditions with great pride.

From my friend's story, I learned that it is important to try to understand and respect other traditions and cultures no matter how different they may be from our own.

# Grandma's Story Telling

In the Niger culture, the life lessons passed on through evening stories told by the village grannies take a very important place in children's education.

It is in the villages where there is no electricity, far away from cars and the busy life and sounds of the city, where after the last prayers and the evening meal, kids gather eagerly around the village grannies before a little campfire, who tell them exciting stories about their ancestors. Tales full of adventure, suspense and other ingredients, that keep the kids frozen while seated on the solid mud floor with their eyes wide open, wishing the story telling would never end.

Here, grandmas are the living memory who with great passion pass on life stories about good and bad, rich and poor, right and wrong, the importance of ancestors, respect for all life, respect for nature and many other rich life lessons. These important life tales have been passed on for many generations, making them very popular and immortal!

# Chapter 4- Holland

## Beautiful Holland....Yummy cheese !!

As cheese is my favorite food, my parents took me to where this beautiful, famous cheese is made. The farm was situated in a lovely countryside location where the scenery was truly awesome with many farms remotely visible behind a hazy curtain of fog, while large flocks of white birds were migrating above the vast Purmer lake.

At this farm we learned how cheese-making goes back hundreds of years in Europe, but also in the Middle East and Central Asia. I would never have thought, as I learned that day, that the production of cheese in Holland was in fact a coincidence discovered when farmers who would take their milk to sell in the marketplace noticed that the milk would start to convert into solid curd which then set the basis for cheese making. This happened due to a key substance called 'rennet' from the stomach of young calves which ended up in the milk because the farmers carried the butchered dairy cattle in the same containers as they carried the milk to the market.

As cheese production in many varieties developed over centuries, Dutch cheese today is very famous and is one of Holland's main exports enjoyed all over the world!

# Dutch Clogs

The Dutch have many nice traditions and customs. Clogs, or 'Klompen', go back to the late 13$^{th}$ century and were the only affordable shoes for most Dutch - many of whom were farmers at the time. They were actually also far more practical and solid than leather shoes in the wet Dutch soil and adapted naturally to the seasonal temperatures.

Clogs are made out of soft popular wood while willow wood is harder but more costly. They were made for different occasions so you could not wear the same type of clog for Sunday church as the one you wore on the farm when attending to farm work, or while attending a festival, or family occasion.

It was funny to learn also that a boy at the time could marry a girl only if he worked hard to carve a beautiful clog and offer it to her parents as a proof to demonstrate his ability to be a capable breadwinner.

What I found to be a very funny and well thought-out trick was that apparently thieves and smugglers used to wear clogs made in such a way that the noses would point in the back and the heel on the front. This was done so that their tracks would mislead the police to the opposite direction! How undeniably genius!

# Words of Thanks

This book was a true pleasure to write and it was an interesting and rewarding journey to see the beautiful final product. When I first thought of sharing my stories, I never thought that so much hard work and determination was involved, and that from writing just a small booklet!

I also realize that this result could never have been achieved without the unconditional support from my dad and mentor Mr. Stanley M.Tilak who always pushes me to do the best I can, my lovely mom who never left my side during the entire process, and the unfailing and invaluable collaboration of my publisher, friends and teachers. In this regard, I wish to express my special thanks to Mr Alexander Zouev who was instrumental in putting the book together. We were also lucky to work with the talented illustrator Ms. Parisa Cheraghi. My sincere thanks to Mr Esmaeil Hosseini Moein, Mr. Mansour Mortezapour, Mr. Bradley Gooding, Mr Kenneth Muller, Ms. Ghanieh Ameripour, Mr Shjaam Ganeshie, Mr Abdul Moktader, Ms. Olga Ferguson, Mr. Aboubacar Maman Gambo, and Ms Louise Donovan for tirelessly proofreading the manuscript and for proposing valuable suggestions.

Their feedback added greatly to the international spirit of this booklet! I am confident that their contribution shall surely be felt by children worldwide through the reading pleasure and the good causes the output of booklet is meant to serve.

Thank you!

Aarush.

CPSIA information can be obtained at www.ICGtesting.com
Printed in the USA
BVIW12n1441271217
503803BV00003B/3